Copyright @2021 by Kwasi Osei-Kuffuor

All rights reserved. No part of this book may be reproduced in any form or by any electronic or mechanical means, including information storage and retrieval systems, without permission in writing from the publisher, except by reviewers, who may quote brief passages in a review.

This publication contains the opinions and ideas of its author. It is intended to provide helpful and informative material on the subjects addressed in the publication. The author and publisher specifically disclaim all responsibility for any liability, loss or risk, personal or otherwise, which is incurred as a consequence, directly or indirectly, of the use and application of any of the contents of this book.

WORKBOOK PRESS LLC
187 E Warm Springs Rd,
Suite B285, Las Vegas, NV 89119, USA

Website: https://workbookpress.com/
Hotline: 1-888-818-4856
Email: admin@workbookpress.com

Ordering Information:
Quantity sales. Special discounts are available on quantity purchases by corporations, associations, and others.
For details, contact the publisher at the address above.

Library of Congress Control Number:
ISBN-13: 978-1-956876-00-0 (Paperback Version)
978-1-956876-01-7 (Digital Version)

REV. DATE: 11/04/2021

Echoes of the Heart

By

Kwasi Osei-Kuffuor

To
Mawusi,
Because you are, I am

A girl like you

How does a girl like you get to be a girl like you?
Fate and chance are never the same
But I will chance my fate with you

What is a girl like you doing in a place like this?
You came into my life like a promised sunrise
And turned my life into an endless song

I DREAM

Through the dark veil of the night
I dream

On the pillows of the mountain peaks
I dream

From the rising of the sun to the setting of the same
I dream
This valley is filled with the season's love.

When the branches of memories sprout
I dream

When promised romance blossoms
I dream

When unspoken words are heard
I dream
This valley is filled with the season's love.

Whether half asleep or awake
I dream

But only for a moment

Like a wonderful dream you came
But only for a moment

Like a forgotten memory you disappeared
But only for a moment

You provoked a hidden desire
But only for a moment

I was drawn to an unknown intoxication
But only for a moment

You turned my sorrow into a song
But only for a moment

Yours is a symphony on my heart's string
But only for a moment

Who are you, who am I?

Who are you?
Where have you been?
I travelled the world to find you
And found you at sun set
Your eyes, like a luminous sunbeam
Told a tale on you
I was never right
You were never wrong
I mistook your affection for romance
You mistook my infatuation for love
Who am I?
Where have I been?

My heart echoes

My heart echoes with mischief
A burning desire
My heart echoes with mischief
A touch of love
You toss your cares away with a wink
And life passes by in a blink
Your love flows like a still river
You see in me
What I see in you.

Romance

With my eyes I see
That I may be seen
With my ears I hear
That I may be heard
With my hands I touch
That I may be touched
With my heart I feel
Your warmth and your coldness
I speak the unspeakable
And pulls your heartstrings
To make you notice me

I tell a little lie
I flatter and l cheat
I make you cry, and sometimes
I even make you laugh
You laugh so loud that you
Are almost blinded by your tears
You call it tears of joy,
I call it forgiveness
Some may even call it love.

I FLY AWAY

I fly away in the open sky
On the wings of your love
I fly away in the open sky
To where my treasure is
Buried deep in a place
Where only you know
So I fly as high as I can
Far ahead of time
The stars smile on me
And I bask in their glow
I fly on the wings of your love
Just to be with you.

Song Bird

The song bird sings a tune or two
And says what is on its mind
Sometimes to me
Sometimes to you
Two souls entwined
A thought and a feeling
Surpassing the fragrance of spring
You feel it and I hear it
In the tune of the song bird

My Love

The Sun shone upon me
And I shine upon the world, my love

The aura of your love envelops me;
A glowing sphere in my life, my love

You walk the fields and the flowers blossom
I submerge in the distant blue sea, my love

Whenever I breathe, I fall for the winds
I am but a weak leaf off your branch, my love

I thirst by the spring waters for a glimpse of you
My heart does not match the heavens, my love

I burn with feverish passion for you
So be my light and chase away the night, my love.

Spread your wings

Spread your wings, give us a chance
Open up to me and stay awhile
As the river meanders through the rustic leaves
So have you snaked your way into my heart
You are lovely

I bask in the shadow of your love
Where I forget myself
You make me feel alive
So blow out the candle light
And give us a chance.

I see you

The night is pleasant
The moon is beautiful
In the moonlighted night I see you
The sun rises and sets on you
The moon illuminates with your smile
Let the pain that leave you sleepless
Burn in the fires of my love

My life, my love

Your essence befits a Woman
My life, my love
Your love turns dust to gold
And melts the hearts of gallant suitors
You wield the power to claim my heart
And your gentleness a soothing balm
You are beautiful

Somewhere in Me

Somewhere in me there life
In you I see a new way of living
You are the reason why I am me
A wish upon a star
Crushed lilies fill up my senses
I die and live a little
Whenever you are near
Do I embrace this happiness?
Do I shed a tear?
I will live and die a little
Just to be with you
I love you.

Moonbeam

You are amazing, oh beloved one
Your enticing gait leads me on
To all the familiar places, where
I breathe moment by moment
In a living daydream

You are the moon amongst the stars
But you put the stars to shade
You are beyond compare
In grace and elegance
Oh beautiful one

I lost my heart when l found you
I lose myself so l could have you
You light up my world
And l grow day by day
You are my moonbeam.

I AM

I am the secret you cannot hide
I am the memory you cannot erase
I am the song that echoes in your heart
So listen to your heart and hear me.

I am the answer to your questions
I am the occupant of your dreams
I am visible in every vision
So open your eyes and see me.

So close to you

I have lost my heart
And now l found happiness
I have been a stranger
And now l found happiness
A bond that that touches the soul
Has drawn me to you
So close to you
But closer to God
In whom love is made perfect.

Your intoxicating ambience
Chases the dark clouds away
And makes the past history
This I cannot deny
So am I drawn close to you
But closer to God
In whom love is made perfect.

The Night is Beautiful

The night is beautiful
Fortune smiles on us
The moonlight is subtle
Hiding your sorrows in its embrace
A million things I want to say to you
But there is a caution in my heart
It will only be a whisper
If only you can trust me.

I am, you are

I am the morning dew, you are my dawn
I am the speaker, you are my prayer
I am the cloud, you are my sky
I am in love, you are my gift
We met, though worlds apart
We shared a dream in a distant past
A dream kept alive by your enduring love
Taking me where I need to be
Thank you for the memory
And the sweet memories you give me.

How do I look to you?

How do I look to you?
Your footsteps ring a bell in my heart
I forget myself whenever you are here
Love me gently
And put this restless soul to rest

How do I look to you?
Your love warms my world
I forget to breathe whenever you are gone
So love me gently
And put this restless soul to rest.

Show me how to love you

Show me how to love you
In your smile you've shown
How you wooed me
In more ways than one
I have loved you
In depth, breath and height

Tell me how to love you
In not so many words you told me
That I needed no other lover
I will love you as freely
As a man strives for righteousness
And purely as a child's faith God above
So show me and tell me.

Meeting you

As the cloud meets the sky
So have I met you!
As the bees meets the buds
So have I met you!
As the rivers flow into the ocean
So am l into you
Come with me, walk with me
The universe has conspired
In love and in life
In love and in a song

My Secret

You have been silent
And l have wondered
How to tell you my secret
I only speak the truth
So ask for my heart, if you may
And lend me your ear
So I can tell you my secret.

LOVE IS...

Love is a delightful burden
Love is a wonderful illness
Sometimes it puts me down
Sometimes it lifts me up
But I will let it grow.

Love is a long friendship
Love is a heart wanting another
Sometimes it makes me laugh
Sometimes it makes me cry
But I will let it grow.

AMAZED

I will stand here and look at you
I see you in every daydream
I close my eyes just to see you
You are amazing

I will stand here and rest my head
In the shelter of your eyes
I will be still and stare
You are a thing to be amazed by.

There is you, there is me

There will be dawn
There will be dusk
The day will pass by
The night will disappear
Flowers will bloom
Even in winter days
Snow will fall in mid-summer
In the Sahara
There has been sun set
There has been sunrise
There has been an eclipse
In the northern hemisphere
And there is you, there is me.

Crazy Heart

It seems to me
That my obsession has been
Misunderstood
There is a scare in my heart
That you will hide away forever
What is the next best thing?
I do not have a clue
So I will hide away awhile
Till your crazy heart finds me

My heart is yours

You are the one I will be thinking of
Yours is the charm that warms my heart
I will find you tomorrow
My heart is yours

You are the one I will be dancing with
Yours is the rhythm that moves my feet
I will love you tomorrow
My heart is yours

You are the one I keep thinking of
Yours is the glitter that beckons to me
I have got to let you know
My heart is yours

Your love is sweet

On a hot summer night
I burn in the rain
Lost in the memory of now
What am I to do?
Your love is sweet

I gaze into your eyes
With a quickening heart
Blinded by your captivating grace
What am I to do?
Your love is sweet

There is excitement in the air
Yet feeling lonesome in crowded places
What am I to do?
Your love is sweet.

Your love, my love

Your love is an addiction
A delightful intoxication
A sweet pain
I fall in, and I fall out
So let it be.

My love is a lovely allure
A playful breeze
A teasing banter
You stay in, and you stay out
So let it be.

I WILL BOLDLY PROCLAIM MY LOVE

I will boldly proclaim my love
There is no privacy in a public place
Commit the folly of loving me back
And fulfil my heart's thrill.

The stars are in love with the sky
Flowers are fated with the morning dew
The thing I most feared has befallen me
And everything has become new

Take a good look at me

Take a good look at me
Don't be shy
Get lost in my arms
Don't be scared
I have waited so long for you
In the warm winter seasons
But spring is now here
April flowers have blossomed
July is awake to summers delight
Leaves are falling in autumn's breeze
In you is nature perfected
So take a good look at me
Don't be shy
Get lost in my arms
And rest awhile.

Echoes of the Heart

You are mine, I am yours
A lover, he whispers
A lover, she hears
And the heart sways
Amidst the sound of silence
It sways ever so gently

A flutter, a wee bit fearful
Yet it sways, ever so slowly
It skips a beat, she trips
It leaps blindly, he falls
The clouds is dense with rain
And flows to a patched desert

She shivers a little
And smiles ever so bashfully
Sometimes at his jokes
And joy, like spring
Pours out of her tender heart

Still my heart, it aches
To hear the rhythm of your feet
Still my heart, it yearns
For your enduring embrace
As a moth is drawn to a flame
So am I drawn to you
You are mine, I am yours.

My heart wonders

Why is there a song in the wind?
Why is the sun raining colours?
My heart wonders

Why is there moonlight in the day?
Why is winter so warm?
My heart wonders

Whose face do I see in the crowd?
Whose voice do I hear in silence?
My heart wonders.

Seasons

I have looked for you for so long
I have yearned for you time after time
What if there is no cloud in the sky?
Or the sun takes a sudden vacation,
I wouldn't care for the outcast sky
Nor if the stars miss a twinkle

It is you who recreates my world
And fills it with endless desire
For you the seasons will be summoned
In unchartered time and space
A year is only a year long
I will be seeing you.

Me, myself and I

I look for you in the night
A rather gloomy ambience
An oasis in an endless desert
A shade in a scorching sun
A balm to a bruised heart

I look for you in the clouds
But you changed into a breeze
I have lived the life of others
But for just one moment
Let me live as me, myself and I

A Reason to Love

Give yourself a reason to love
Being so close, yet so far apart
There is a longing to belong
We met somewhere here
And belong somewhere there
Feelings have risen from within
Buried in the labyrinth of my soul
Free as a kite, I am
Swift as a falcon, you are
So give yourself a reason to love

Mawusi

Like the sun you spread your warmth
And the lonesome cold nights disappears
With each burst of energy
I have loved you in every lifetime
As you learnt fragrance to my breath

To the garden you have brought spring
And the Sahara is no longer deprived
You love me as you love yourself
And trust me more than I do myself

With you the path has been clearer
And the journey made easier
Without you there is nothing else
Because you are, I am.

www.ingramcontent.com/pod-product-compliance
Lightning Source LLC
Chambersburg PA
CBHW072040080526
44578CB00007B/538